AN INDEX OF L HOSPITALS AND THEIR RECORDS

Compiled by Cliff Webb

SOCIETY OF GENEALOGISTS ENTERPRISES LTD

Published by
Society of Genealogists Enterprises Limited
14 Charterhouse Buildings
Goswell Road
London EC1M 7BA

First Edition 2002
Reprinted 2008

© C R Webb

ISBN 10: 1-903462-88-6
ISBN 13: 978-1-903462-88-1

British Library Cataloguing in Publication Data

A CIP Catalogue record for this book is available from the British Library

Cover Image - St. George's Hospital, about 1750.

CONTENTS

INTRODUCTION

Hospital records are an extremely useful source of information. However, many records are not yet available for consultation. There are various rules and closure periods, however in general any record containing details about patients is closed for 100 years after the last entry. However, religious records such as baptism registers in hospital chapels are not closed at all. This leads to the rather absurd situation that baptism records are always open, while birth records are only open after 100 years. There are very few burial registers for hospitals; almost all are death registers, thus suffering from this extended closure period.

There has been, as is almost inevitable in a pioneering work of this nature, a problem defining classes of records. Varying record listers will list identical matter under different headings.

The most generally genealogically useful of hospital records (other than vital records of birth, baptism and death) are admission and discharge registers. These may give all sorts of information, including, vitally, age, address and sometimes next of kin. Creed registers (unfortunately subject to the 100 years closure rules) are effectively birth records. Staff records can also be extremely useful usually giving at the time of appointment age and address. Occasionally, records exist of pensions, etc. which may give date of death.

Substantial help has been received from the Wellcome Trust/Public Record Office database of hospital records.

Alexandra Hospital for Children with Hip Disease, Southampton Row, WC1. Opened 1866.

Annual reports 1897-1938 (LMA: SC/PPS)

All Saint's Hospital see Westminster Hospital Urological Centre

All Saint's Hospital for Genito-Urinary Diseases see Westminster Hospital Urological Centre

Annie Mccall Maternity Hospital, Jeffrey's Road, SW4 (LMA: H24/AM). Opened as Clapham Maternity Hospital, 1889. Renamed 1935. Closed 1970.

Baptisms 1924-40, 1945-69 (LMA: P95/JNE1); Baptisms at St John's House, Battersea 1886-92 (LMA: H1/ST/SJ); annual reports 1899-1952 (LMA: SC/PPS)

Anti-Vivisection Hospital see Battersea General Hospital

Archway Hospital, Archway Road, N19. Opened 1879 as Holborn Union Infirmary; renamed 1921as Holborn and Finsbury Hospital; renamed 1930, Archway Hospital. Absorbed into Whittington Hospital, 1952.

Baby Clinic and Hospital, Ladbroke Square, W11. Opened c1911. Closed 1948.

Annual reports 1921-1938 (LMA: SC/PPS)

Battersea General Hospital, Prince of Wales Road, SW11. (LMA: HO6/BG). Founded as National Anti-Vivisection Hospital in 1896 and known as the Anti-Vivisection Hospital, Battersea General Hospital from 1910 and from 1935 as Battersea General Hospital. Became part of Battersea, Putney and Tooting Group. Closed 1972.

minute books 1905-71 (LMA); annual reports 1904-47 (LMA: SC/PPS)

Bearsted Memorial Hospital, Lordship Road, N16. Opened in Underwood Street, Whitechapel, E1 as Jewish Maternity, District Nursing and Sickness Help Society, 1895; Jewish Maternity Home 1929-37; moved and renamed 1937/8; closed 1980.

Annual reports 1915-47 (LMA: SC/PPS)

Bedlam see Bethlem Royal Hospital

Belgrave Hospital for Children, 1 Clapham Road, SW9. Opened 1866. Absorbed in King's College Hospital (King's College Hospital and LMA).

Administrative records 1903-48 (LMA); annual reports 1898-1947 (LMA: SC/PPS)
Clinical and patient records 1903-48 (King's College Hospital)

Bermondsey and Rotherhithe Hospital and Bermondsey and Rotherhithe Infirmary see St Olave's Hospital

Bermondsey Medical Mission Hospital (for Women and Children), Grange Road, SE1. Opened 1904; now closed.

Annual reports 1926-47 (LMA: SC/PPS)

Bethlem Royal Hospital, Monks Orchard Road, Beckenham, Kent. Opened as The Priory of St Mary of Bethlehem (or Our Lady of Bethlehem), in Bishopsgate, 1247; moved to Moorfields, 1676; to St George's Fields, Southwark, 1815; to Beckenham, 1930.

A&R 1683; clinical records 1816-1948; minute books 1559-1950; staff records 1777 (Hospital); annual reports 1955-60 (LMA: SC/PPS)

Bethnal Green Hospital, Cambridge Heath Road, E2. Opened as Bethnal Green Workhouse Infirmary 1900; renamed 1928; closed 1990 (LMA and Royal London Hospital Archives Centre and Museum)

A&D 1900-18; Administrative records 1900-48; staff records 1914-30 (LMA) A&D 1962-74; staff records 1919-70; nursing records 1906-69; Administrative records 1900-90 (Royal London Hospital Archives Centre)

Blackheath and Charlton Hospital, Shooter's Hill Road, SE3. Opened 1880 as Blackheath and Charlton Cottage Hospital; renamed 1909.

Annual reports 1902-40 (LMA: SC/PPS)

Bolingbroke Hospital, Wakehurst Road, Wandsworth Common, SW11 (LMA and Bolingbroke Hospital. Opened 1880.

A&D 1912-29; Administrative records 1891-1989 (Bolingbroke Hospital)

Annual reports 1897-1947 (LMA: SC/PPS)

Borough of Wandsworth Babies Hospital, Leigham Court Road, SW16.

Annual reports 1940-43 (LMA: SC/PPS)

British Dental Hospital, Bloomsbury. Opened in Camden Road, NW1 c1911.

Annual reports 1927-29, 1943, 1946 (LMA: SC/PPS)

British Hospital for Mothers and Babies, Woolwich, SE18 (LMA: H14/BMB). The Home for Mothers and Babies opened in 1905 in two converted houses. It merged with the British Lying-in Hospital, Holborn in 1915, which itself closed in 1913 and the Home renamed British Hospital for Mothers and Babies. A site in Samuel Street, Woolwich was purchased in 1914, and a new Hospital opened in 1922. It was damaged in 1940 by enemy action, and temporary hospitals were located at Chesham, Buckinghamshire and Brenchley, Kent. It was taken over by the National Health Service in 1948 and closed in 1984.

Diaries (incl. A&D) 1905-45; registers of patients 1947-58; casebooks 1905-09, 1912-48; maternity register 1949; medical report books 1933-47; outpatients casebooks 1939, 1946; midwives 1906-19; minute books 1904-72; annual reports 1906-49, 1968-69; letters 1939-45; donations 1911-20; visitors 1905-29, 1948-61 (LMA)

British Lying-in Hospital, Endell Street, Holborn, WC2 (LMA: H14/BLI and PRO). Founded in 1749 in Brownlow Street, Long Acre as the Lying-in Hospital for Married Women. Renamed 1756, moved to Endell Street, 1849. Closed 1913 and amalgamated with the Home for Mothers and Babies, Woolwich which was renamed the British Hospital for Mothers and Babies.

Births 1749-1868 (PRO: RG8); Administrative records 1749-1868 (PRO) Delivery book 1856-60; casebooks 1905-09 (casebooks 1767-80 are in Library of Royal College of Obstetricians and Gynaecologists); minute books 1749-1860, 1869-1914; annual reports 1880-1909; accounts 1808-20 (LMA); annual reports 1897-1912 (LMA: SC/PPS)

Brixton Dispensary, The Crypt, St Matthew's Church, SW2 (Lambeth Archives Department). Opened as Brixton, Streatham Hill and Herne Hill General Dispensary in Water Lane, Brixton, 1850; renamed 1923; moved 1944; closed 1948 and funds used to supply food etc. to sick poor.

Administrative and general records 1945-1973 (Lambeth Archives Department)

Brook General Hospital, Shooters Hill Road, Woolwich, SE18 (LMA: H20/BK). Opened 1896 as a hospital for infectious diseases. Closed 1995.
Baptisms 1962-94, Deaths 1904-08; A&D 1897-1926, 1930-33, 1940, 1953-57; Creed registers 1933-35, 1942-43; registers of patients 1941-50; casebooks 1929-49; operations 1953-63; staff

records 1926-30; list of nurses 1955-74; chapel service registers 1977-95 (LMA)

Camberwell House Asylum, Peckham Road, SE5. Opened 1846; closed 1955.

Clinical records 1847-87 (Wellcome Institute)

Camberwell Workhouse Infirmary and Camberwell Parish Infirmary see St Giles' Hospital

Cancer Hospital see Royal Marsden Hospital

Central London Opthalmic Hospital, Judd Street, WC1. Opened 1843; closed 1948.

Annual reports 1897-1946 (LMA: SC/PPS)

Central London Throat, Nose and Ear Hospital see Royal National Throat Nose and Ear Hospital

Charing Cross Hospital, Agar Street, W2, later Fulham Palace Road, W6. Opened 1818.

minute books 1818-1979; nurses 1858-1971; clinical records 1885-1923 (Hospital); annual reports 1897-1947, 1953-56, 1961-3 (LMA: SC/PPS)

Chartham Park Convalescent Home see Westminster Hospital

Chelsea Hospital for Women,
Goldhawk Road, W6. (LMA: H27/CW and H27/QC) Founded 1871 in Kings

Road; moved to Fulham Road, 1883 and to Arthur Street in 1916 which was renamed Dovehouse Street in 1939. Closed and transferred to Queen Charlotte Hospital, Goldhawk Road, 1988

Baptisms 1837; A&D 1948-51, 1957-58; minute books 1872-1950; Matrons reports 1930-62; medical registers 1895-1948; casebooks 1872-1948; staff records 1899-1961; visitors 1895-1957 (LMA); annual reports 1898-1947 (LMA: SC/PPS)
A&D 1894-1968; minute books 1880-1968; clinical records 1884-1980; staff records 1890-1930 (Hospital)

Chelsea Pensioners' Hospital see Royal Hospital

Chelsea Workhouse Infirmary see St Luke's Hospital

Cheyne Hospital for Sick and Incurable Children, Cheyne Walk, SW3. Opened 1875; renamed Cheyne Hospital, 1908; closed 1955

annual reports 1898-1947 (LMA:

SC/PPS); estate and administrative records 1712-1947 (LMA)

Child Psychiatric Day Hospital, Black Prince Road, SE11. Opened 1914; from 1924-35 known as St Thomas Cornwall Babies' Hostel, Prince's Road, SE11; from 1935 to 1968 known as St Thomas' Babies' Hostel; evacuated to Wiltshire during war and moved after 1945; closed 1990. (LMA: H1/ST/CH)

Children's Hospital, Hampstead see Hospital and Home for Incurable Children

Children's Hospital, Sydenham Road, Lewisham, SE26. Opened 1872 as South Eastern Hospital for Children; from 1950 to c1960 Sydenham Babies Hospital.

minute books, etc. 1872-1942 (Lewisham Local Studies Centre)
minute books, etc. 1881-1978 (Lewisham Hospital)
Annual reports 1902-47 (LMA)

City of London Hospital for Diseases of the Chest see London Chest Hospital

City Lying-in Hospital see City of London Maternity Hospital

City of London Maternity Hospital, Hanley Road, Islington, N4. Opened 1750 in Aldersgate Street as City Lying-in Hospital (renamed 1918); moved to City Road and Old Street, 1773 and in 1949 to Hanley Road (LMA: H10/CLM)
See: City of London Maternity Hospital, A short history (Ralph B. Cannings, 1922)

Baptisms 1813-1978; A&D 1750-69, 1861-1948; outpatients A&D 1872-1953; matrons' casebooks 1921-49; district casebooks 1913-42; governor's minute books 1750-56, 1767-1948; letters of recommendation 1788, 1814, 1822; legacies 1754-1830, 1927-65 (LMA); annual reports 1900-46 (LMA: SC/PPS)

City of London Union Infirmary, Clifden Road, E9. Opened 1910 as City of London Workhouse; closed 1920 and amalgamated with Eastern Hospital; from 1927 Thavies Inn Infirmary; absorbed by Sheffield Street Hospital, 1931.

A&D 1911-14; minute books 1910-14 (LMA: Board of Guardians records)

City of London Workhouse, City of London Infirmary, City of London, Bow Institution see St Clement's Hospital

City of Westminster Hospital see St Stephen's Hospital

City Orthopaedic Hospital, Hatton Garden, EC4. Opened 1851; closed 1907. No records known to survive apart from a few annual reports 1898-1905 at LMA.

Clapham Maternity Hospital see Annie Mccall Maternity Hospital

Cleveland Street Children's Infirmary, Cleveland Street, NW1. Opened 1876; closed 1922.

A&D 1875-1930; minute books 1875-1930; staff records 1916-22 (LMA: Holborn, Westminster and St Pancras Boards of Guardians Records)

Constance Road Institution see St Francis' Hospital

Dental Hospital, Mortimer Market, WC1. Also at Great Portland Street and Devonshire Street, W1. Opened 1861 as National Dental Hospital; renamed 1963. minute books 1877-1964; clinical records 1922-31; staff records 1926-64 (University College Hospital) minute books 1901-14 (LMA)

Dental Hospital of London see Royal Dental Hospital

Deptford Hospital see New Cross Hospital

Deptford Medical Mission and Convalescent Home, High Street, Deptford, SE8. Opened 1889.

Annual reports 1909-14 (LMA: SC/PPS)

Dispensary for Women and Children see Queen Elizabeth Hospital for Children

Dreadnought Seamen's Hospital, King William Walk, Greenwich, SE10. Founded in a ship called the Grampus in 1821 which replaced the Dreadnought in 1831. In 1870, the Hospital moved onshore into the old Greenwich Infirmary. Closed 1986.
See: The History of the Dreadnought Seamen's Hospital at Greenwich (A.G. McBride)

A&D 1826-1977; clinical records 1914-50; minute books 1826-1977 (National Maritime Museum, Manuscripts Section) Deaths 1949-86; A&D 1977-86; operations 1971-86; minute books 1945-74; visitors 1929-43 (LMA: H51) records of nurses 1920-30, minute books 1920-30 (Nursing Department, Greenwich District Hospital)

Dulwich Hospital, East Dulwich Grove, SE22. Opened 1886 as St Saviour's Union Infirmary; renamed Southwark Hospital 1921; renamed Dulwich Hospital, 1931.

A&D 1825-1972; clinical records 1892-1970; minute books 1825-1972; staff records 1893-1947 (Dulwich Hospital) minute books 1887-1948; staff records 1887-1920 (LMA)

East End Maternity Hospital, Commercial Road, E1. Opened 1884 as Mothers' Lying-In Home; renamed 1902 East End Mothers' Home; 1903 East End Mothers' Lying-In Home; 1926 East End Maternity Hospital; closed 1968.

A&D 1884-1968; minute books 1884-1968; records of nurses 1924-41 (Royal London Hospital Archives Centre and Museum); annual reports 1898-1947 (LMA: SC/PPS)

Eastern Dispensary, Leman Street, E1. Opened in Great Alie Street, Whitechapel, 1782; moved 1858; closed 1940.

minute books 1808-1952 (Royal London Hospital Archives Centre and Museum)

Eastern Hospital, Homerton Grove, E9. Opened 1867 as Homerton Hospital or Metropolitan Fever and Smallpox Hospitals at Homerton; renamed 1885 as Eastern Fever Hospital; 1899 Eastern Hospital; closed 1982.

A&D 1897-1916; minute books 1868-1968; staff records 1871-1924 (LMA); annual reports 1875-85 (LMA: SC/PPS) A&D 1885-1927; clinical records 1871-1980 minute books 1739-1972; staff records 1874-1938 (St Bartholomew's Hospital Archives and Museum)

East London Hospital for Children, Glamis Road, Stepney, E1. Renamed Princess Elizabeth of York Hospital for Children, 1932.

Annual reports 1897-1941 (LMA: SC/PPS)

Eastman Dental Hospital, Grays Inn Road, WC1. Opened 1948.

minute books 1930-48 (Hospital)

Elizabeth Garrett Anderson Hospital, Euston Road, NW1. Elizabeth Garrett Anderson opened St Mary's Dispensary in Bryanston Square, St Marylebone in 1866, which became known as the New Hospital for Women in 1872. In 1874 it moved to the Marylebone Road and in 1889 to Euston Road. The Hospital was renamed after its founder after her death in 1917. In 1948 the Hospital opened the Garrett Anderson Maternity Home in Belsize Grove, Hampstead. The early records were transferred to the Public Record Office before 1980, but to London Metropolitan Archives in 1984. See: Elizabeth Garrett Anderson 1836-1917 (L.G. Anderson, 1939); Elizabeth Garrett Anderson (J. Manton, 1965)

A&D 1946-49; registers of patients 1906-25; casebooks 1948-52; minute books 1871-1967; staff records 1898-1948; annual reports 1873-1968; bequests 1885-1954; visitors 1913-63 (LMA: H13/EGA)

Eltham and Mottingham Hospital, Passey Place, Woolwich, SE9. Opened c1869; closed 1983.

Annual reports 1902-47 (LMA: SC/PPS)

Evelina Hospital for Children,
Southwark Bridge Road, SE1 (LMA:
H9/EV).
See: The Evelina. The Story of a London
Children's Hospital 1869-1969 (H.E.
Priestly, 1969)

Baptisms 1935-75; Deaths 1908-12; post-
mortems 1892-97, 1908-17, 1930-48;
casualty registers 1907, 1912-13, 1917-
20, 1924, 1927-28, 1931-33, 1837-43,
1947-48; casebooks 1874-77, 1889-1904,
1911-39; registers of patients 1918-26;
reports on patients 1936-38; clinical
records 1869-1912; operations 1909-14,
1929-40; registers of nurses 1896-1914;
staff records 1875, 1888-1949; minute
books 1869-1948; donations 1881-82,
1893-1939; visitors 1867-1919
Annual reports 1898-1947 (LMA:
SC/PPS)

**Florence Nightingale Hospital for
Gentlewomen**, Lisson Grove, St
Marylebone, NW1. Opened in Harley
Street in 1850 as Hospital for Invalided
Gentlewomen; renamed 1909; closed
1948.

Bequests 1930-46; annual reports 1913,
1920-49; letters 1937-48; deeds 1892-
1938 (LMA: H54); annual reports 1903-
47, 1954-58 (LMA: SC/PPS)

Fountain Hospital, Tooting Grove,
SW17. Opened 1893 as Fountain Fever
Hospital; renamed 1912; closed 1963
A&D 1897-1930; minute books 1893-
1948 (LMA)

Free Hospital see Royal Free Hospital

Free Hostel for the Dying see Hostel of
God

**French Hospital and Dispensary and
French Convalescent Home**,
Shaftesbury Avenue, WC2. Opened 1867;
closed 1948.

Annual reports 1898-1947, 1960 (LMA:
SC/PPS)

Friedenheim Hospital see St Columba's
Hospital

Fulham Hospital see Western Hospital

Fulham Maternity Hospital, Parson's
Green, SW6. Opened 1915 as Fulham
Borough Maternity Home; closed 1970.

A&D 1937-68; clinical records 1937-68;
minute books 1937-68 (Hammersmith
and Fulham Archives)

Fulham Hospital, St Dunstan's Road,
W6. Opened 1884 as Fulham Parish
Infirmary; Fulham Infirmary 1922-25
and St Christopher's Hospital 1926-28.
Closed.

A&D 1884-1927; minute books 1877-
1948; staff records 1884-86; annual
reports 1877-82 (LMA)
A&D 1955-71; minute books 1955-71
(Charing Cross Hospital)
Fulham Road Infirmary see St Stephen's
Hospital

Garrett Anderson Maternity Home see
Elizabeth Garrett Anderson Hospital

General Lying-in Hospital see Queen Charlotte's Maternity Hospital

General Lying-in Hospital, York Road, Lambeth, SE1 (LMA: HI/GLI; P85/MRY1/) opened 1767 as Westminster New Lying-in Hospital, Westminster Bridge Road, Lambeth; change of name 1818. Relief for poor women especially wives of soldiers and sailors. Moved to York Road, 1828. Evacuated to St Albans 1939-46. See: *A Brief History of the General Lying-in Hospital*, 1965

baptisms 1794-1872 (LMA: in P85/MRY1); 1872-1918 (LMA: HI/GLI/B15/1-4); A&D 1767-1944, 1950-51; affidavits (give settlement) 1816-40; minute books 1765-1955; registers of patients 1887-1966; registers of outpatients 1877-82, 1900-18; midwives day and casebooks 1824-1900, 1909-10, 1946-71; casebooks 1827-1947; annual reports 1879-1947; staff records 1879-1970; visitors' book 1865-1907

German Hospital, Ritson Road (and Dalston Lane), E8. Opened 1845; closed 1987.

A&D 1946-67; clinical records 1931-59; minute books 1802-1971; staff records 1845-1955 (St Bartholomew's Hospital Archives)
Annual reports 1898-1947 (LMA: SC/PPS)

Golden Square Throat Nose and Ear Hospital, Golden Square, W1. Opened 1863 as Hospital for Diseases of the Throat; closed 1948 when became a teaching hospital.

Annual reports 1898-1939 (LMA: SC/PPS)

Goldie Leigh Hospital, Lodge Hill, SE2. Opened 1914; known as Goldie Leigh Homes 1916-33.

A&D 1902-20; minute books 1902-48; staff records 1914-32 (LMA)

Gordon Hospital, Vauxhall Bridge Road, SW1. Opened 1864 as the Western Hospital for Fistula, Piles and Other Diseases of the Rectum; renamed Gordon Hospital for Rectal Diseases, 1911, Gordon Hospital for Diseases of the Rectum and Colon, 1939 and the Gordon Hospital, 1941

A&D 1937-49; registers of patients 1937-49, 1956-58; minute books 1884-1968; annual reports 1885-1947; staff records 1920s-50s

Great Northern Hospital and Great Northern Central Hospital see Royal Northern Hospital

Great Ormond Street Hospital see Hospital for Children

Greenwich District Hospital, Vanbrugh Hill, SE10. Opened 1874 as Greenwich Union Infirmary; renamed 1928 as Greenwich and Deptford Hospital; St Alfege's Hospital 1931-68.

A&D 1874-1942; minute books 1874-1951; staff records 1904-29 (LMA: H43) clinical records 1948-86; minute books 1948-86 (Hospital)

Grosvenor Hospital for Women, Vincent Square, SW1.

A&D 1921-62; minute books 1877-1951; operations 1968-71; annual reports 1874-75, 1886-1948; letters 1897, 1931-41; operations 1968-71 (LMA: HI/G); annual reports 1897-1947 (LMA: SC/PPS)

Grove Hospital, Tooting Grove, SW17. Opened as Grove Fever Hospital 1899; renamed 1948; closed 1958.

A&D 1897-1916; minute books 1897-1948; staff records 1899-1914 (LMA) minute books 1899-1954; staff records 1899-1954 (St Georges Hospital Medical School Library)

Grove Park Hospital, Marvels Lane, SE12. Opened 1906 as Grove Park Workhouse; renamed 1918 after wartime use as Army Service Corps HQ. Only part of the grounds of this Hospital were within the L.C.C. district.

A&D 1904-14; minute books 1896-1993; staff records 1901-35 (LMA: H39/GP) minute books 1920-74; clinical records 1960-80; staff records 1940-60 (Hospital)

Guy's Hospital, St Thomas' Street, SE1. Opened 1725. (LMA: H9/GY) See: Guy's Hospital. A Brief Account of the Origin, Past History and Present Work of a Great Institution (1925); Guy's Hospital 1725-1948 (H.A. Ripman, 1951); A Short Bibliographical History of Guy's Hospital (F.N. Doubleday, 1951); A Brief History of Guy's Hospital (G.A.R. Winson & W.H. Hills, 1952); Mr Guy's Hospital 1726-1948 (H.C.

Cameron, 1954); Guy's Hospital, A Short Account of Nursing 1725-1968 (1968); The First Matron of Guy's Hospital and her staff (P. Edden, 1968); Guy's Hospital Chapel: A short history (1980)

Baptisms 1888-1938; Deaths 1726-1946; A&D 1725-1948; indexes of patients 1809-1939; minute books 1725-1948; Matrons reports 1892-1939; registers of probationers 1928-54; staff records 1890-1960; endowments 1725-1944; chapel services 1888-1967; apprenticeship records 1727-32 (LMA); annual reports 1897-1947 (LMA: SC/PPS)

A&D 1776-1816; minute books 1776-1816 (Southwark Local Studies Library)

Hackney Hospital, Homerton High Street, E9. Opened 1750 as Hackney Workhouse Infirmary; Hackney Union Infirmary 1874-1930; Hackney Institution 1930-48. Closed 1995.

A&D 1881-85; clinical records 1876-1983; minute books 1879-1948; staff records 1899-1930 (LMA) A&D 1880-81; clinical records 1876-1983; minute books 1788-1967 (St Bartholomew's Hospital Archives)

Hammersmith Hospital, Du Cane Road, W12. Opened 1905 as Hammersmith Board of Guardians Infirmary; renamed Hammersmith Institution and Infirmary 1927; Hammersmith Hospital, 1930. A&D 1906-35; clinical records 1930-69; minute books 1906-61 (LMA: H37/HM); annual reports 1957-61 (LMA: SC/PPS) clinical records 1934-41 (Royal College of Physicians)

Hampstead Asylum see North Western Hospital

Hampstead Fever and Smallpox Hospital, NW3.

Annual report 1875 (LMA: SC/PPS)

Hampstead General Hospital, Haverstock Hill, NW3. Opened 1882 in South Hill Park Road as Hampstead Home Hospital and Nursing Institute; moved and renamed c1906; closed 1975.

clinical records 1910-75; minute books 1882-1974; staff records 1925 (Royal Free Hospital Archives Centre); annual reports 1898-1947 (LMA: SC/PPS)

Hampstead Hospital see North Western Hospital

Hampstead Hospital for Children see Hospital and Home for Incurable Children

Hampstead Union Workhouse see New End Hospital

Hereford Lodge, Pembridge Square, Bayswater, W2. Opened 1893 as St Luke's Hospital for the Dying; closed 1984.

clinical records 1896-1965; minute books 1891-1971; staff records 1912-45 (St Mary's Hospital Archives)
Annual reports 1904-47 (LMA: SC/PPS)

Highgate Hospital, Dartmouth Park Hill, N19. Opened 1868 as Highgate Infirmary; St Pancras' North Infirmary 1883-1922. Closed.

A&D 1868-1932; minute books 1868-1948; staff records 1882-1930 (LMA)

Hither Green Hospital, Hither Green Lane, SE13. Opened as Park Fever Hospital 1897; Park Hospital 1948-57.

minute books 1894-1976; staff records 1897-1976 (LMA: H41/HG)
A&D 1898-1966; clinical records 1897-1972; minute books 1879-1978; staff records 1897-1978 (Hospital)

Holborn and Finsbury Institution and Holborn and Finsbury Workhouse see St Matthew's Hospital

Home and Infirmary for Sick Children see Children's Hospital, Lewisham.

Home Hospitals Association (For Paying Patients), Fitzroy Square, W1. Opened 1877.

minute books 1920-43 (LMA)

Home for Mothers and Babies see British Hospital for Mothers and Babies
Home of Peace see St Columba's Hospital

Homerton Hospital see Eastern Hospital

Hospital and Home for Incurable Children, College Crescent, Hampstead, NW3. Opened c1875, renamed Northcourt Hospital and Home for Sick Children, 1920, Hampstead Hospital for Children, 1929, Children's Hospital, Hampstead, 1930.

Annual reports 1899-1947 (LMA: SC/PPS)

Hospital and Home for Incurables see Royal Hospital and Home

Hospital for Children, Great Ormond Street, Bloomsbury, WC1. Opened 1852 as Hospital for Sick Children. Colloquially known as Great Ormond Street Hospital.

A&D 1852-1990; clinical records 1852-1990; minute books 1850-1990; staff records 1852-1990 (Hospital)
Annual reports 1897-1947 (LMA: SC/PPS)

Hospital for Consumption and Diseases of the Chest see Royal Brompton National Heart and Lung Hospital

Hospital for Diseases of the Heart see National Heart Hospital

Hospital for Diseases of the Skin, Blackfriars Road, SE1. Opened in London Wall 1841 as London Infirmary for the Cure of Diseases of the Skin; moved to Bridge Street, Blackfriars and renamed London Cutaneous Infirmary 1844; London Cutaneous Institution for Treatment and Cure of Non-Infectious Diseases of the Skin 1845-50; Closed 1953.

minute books 1842-1945; annual reports 1910-25 (LMA)
Hospital for Diseases of the Throat see Golden Square Throat Nose and Ear Hospital

Hospital for Epilepsy and Paralysis and other Diseases of the Nervous System

see Maida Vale Hospital for Nervous Diseases

Hospital for Invalided Gentlewomen see Florence Nightingale Hospital for Gentlewomen

Hospital of St John and St Elizabeth, Grove End Road, St John's Wood, NW8. Opened 1856 in Great Ormond Street; moved 1898; closed 1948.

Annual reports 1898-1950 (LMA: SC/PPS)

Hospital for Sick Children see Hospital for Children

Hospital for Women, Soho Square, W1. Opened in Red Lion Square, 1842 as Hospital for Diseases of Women, 1842; renamed 1846; moved 1852 to Soho Square; closed.

A&D 1922-50; clinical records 1922-50; minute books 1842-1956 (Middlesex Hospital Archives Department)
Annual reports 1897-1947 (LMA: SC/PPS)

Hostel of God, North Side, Clapham Common, SW4. Opened 1891 as Free Home or Hostel for the Dying; closed 1981.

Annual reports 1903, 1925-30, 1932-37, 1945, 1950 (LMA: SC/PPS)

Hostel of St Luke – The Clergy Nursing Home, Fitzroy Avenue, W1. Opened 1892; closed 1948.

Annual reports 1910-47 (LMA: SC/PPS)
Infants' Hospital, The see Westminster
Children's Hospital

Infirmary for Asthma, Consumption and
other Pulmonary Diseases see Royal
Chest Hospital

Infirmary for Relief of the Poor Afflicted
With Fistula and other Diseases of the
Rectum see St Mark's Hospital for
Diseases of the Rectum and Colon

Institution for the cure and prevention of
contagious fevers see Royal Free
Hospital Liverpool Road Branch

**Invalid Asylum and Stoke Newington
Home Hospital for Women**, Stoke
Newington High Street, N16. Opened
1829, renamed Stoke Newington Home
Hospital for Women, 1915.

Annual reports 1904, 1913-43 (LMA:
SC/PPS)

Italian Hospital, Queen Square,
Bloomsbury, WC1. Opened 1884; closed
1948.

Annual reports 1898-1956 (LMA:
SC/PPS)

Ivy House (Maternity) Hospital see
Mothers' Hospital of the Salvation Army

Jewish Home of Rest, Birchlands
Avenue, Wandsworth, SW12. Opened
1895.

Annual reports 1930-47 (LMA: SC/PPS)

Jewish Maternity, District Nursing and
Sickness Help Society and Jewish
Maternity Home see Bearsted Memorial
Hospital

Kensington Dispensary and Children's
Hospital see Princess Louise Hospital for
Children

Kensington General Hospital and in 1909
as Kensington and Fulham General
Hospital see Princess Beatrice Hospital

Kensington Infirmary see St Mary
Abbot's Hospital

Kent Dispensary see Miller General
Hospital

**King Edward VII's Hospital for
Officers**, Grosvenor Crescent, W1.

Annual reports 1924-37 (LMA: SC/PPS)

King's College Hospital, Denmark Hill,
Camberwell, SE5. Opened in Portugal
Street, 1840; moved 1913.
A&D 1860-1914; clinical records 1840-
1937; minute books 1831-1948; staff
records 1860-1914 (Hospital)
Annual reports 1897-1947 (LMA:
SC/PPS)

Kirchner Convalescent Home, Sea
Copse Hill, Wootton, Isle of Wight.
Given to Royal Waterloo Hospital in
1914; sold 1924. (LMA: HI/RW/K)
A&D 1914-24; minute books 1914-24

Lambeth Hospital, Brook Drive, SE11. (LMA: HI/L and La.BG) Originated in Renfrew Road Workhouse which opened 1871 and Lambeth Infirmary opened 1876 on adjoining site in Brook Drive. Renamed Lambeth Hospital, 1922 and became part of St Thomas' Hospital Group, 1964. Closed 1976 on opening of north wing of St Thomas'.
See: Lambeth Hospital Fifty Years Retrospect (P.J. Watkin, c1951)

Births 1914-48; Deaths 1869-1947; Burials 1890-1929; Mortuary registers 1935-64; A&D 1877, 1899-1948; Creed registers 1878-1948; minute books 1948-76; treatment books 1900-03, 1908-10; registers of patients 1928-51; lunatics 1889-1931; registers of maternity patients 1927-38, 1951-54, 1957-61; casebooks 1912-49; operations 1927-30; letters 1913-34; staff records 1867-1917 (in LMA: La.BG.229/1-7); registers of nurses 1957-1958

Lewisham Hospital, High Street, SE13. Opened as Lewisham Workhouse 1817; renamed 1894.

A&D 1894-1922; minute books 1894-1948; staff records 1894-1930 (LMA) clinical records 1944-70; minute books 1832-1977 (Lewisham Local Studies Centre)

Lock Hospital see London Lock Hospital

London Chest Hospital, Bonner Road, Victoria Park, E2. Opened 1848 as City of London Hospital for Diseases of the Chest; renamed 1936.

clinical records 1890-1946 (Royal College of Physicians)

Annual reports 1897-1947 (LMA: SC/PPS)

London Cutaneous Infirmary and London Cutaneous Institution for Treatment and Cure of Non-Infectious Diseases of the Skin see Hospital for Diseases of the Skin

London Dental Hospital, Leicester Square, WC2.

minute books 1864-1901 (City of Westminster Archives Centre)

London Fever Hospital see Royal Free Hospital Liverpool Road Branch

London Foot Hospital, Fitzroy Square, W1. Opened 1913.

Annual report 1936 (LMA: SC/PPS)

London General Institution for the Gratuitous Cure of Malignant Diseases see Royal Free Hospital

London Homeopathic Hospital see Royal London Homeopathic Hospital

London Hospital, Bancroft Road, E1. Opened 1858 as Mile End Old Town Workhouse; renamed Mile End Old Town Infirmary, 1881; renamed Mile End Hospital, 1929

A&D 1900-25; clinical records 1928-47; minute books 1879-1952 (LMA: H21/ME); annual reports 1897-1947 (LMA: SC/PPS)
minute books 1880-1989 (Royal London Hospital Archives Centre)

London Hospital (St Clement's) see St Clement's Hospital

London Hospital (Whitechapel), Whitechapel Road, E1. Opened 1740 in Featherstone Street as The London Infirmary; in Prescot Street 1741-57; renamed The London Hospital, c1748; renamed the London Hospital (Whitechapel), 1968.

A&D 1760-1946; clinical records 1893-1986; minute books 1740-1991; staff records 1880-1940 (Royal London Hospital Archives Centre)
clinical records 1905-65 (Wellcome Institute)

London Infirmary see London Hospital (Whitechapel)

London Infirmary for the Cure of Diseases of the Skin see Hospital for Diseases of the Skin

London Jewish Hospital, Stepney Green, E1. Opened 1907; closed 1979

minute books 1919-80 (Royal London Hospital Archives Centre)
Annual reports 1915-47 (LMA: SC/PPS)

London Lock Hospital and Home, Harrow Road, W9 and Dean Street, Soho, W1. Opened 1746 in Grosvenor Place; moved Harrow Road in (female) 1842 and Dean Street (male) 1862; closed 1948.

clinical records 1849-51; minute books 1746-1948 (Royal College of Surgeons)
Annual reports 1896-1947 (LMA: SC/PPS)

London Skin Hospital, Fitzroy Square, W1. Opened in Cranbourne Street, 1887; moved 1891.

Annual reports 1908-25 (LMA: SC/PPS)

London Temperance Hospital see National Temperance Hospital

London Throat Hospital for Diseases of the Throat, Nose and Ear, Great Portland Street and Bolsover Street, W1. Opened 1872; now closed.

Annual reports 1899-1913 (LMA: SC/PPS)

Lying-in Hospital for Married Women see British Lying-in Hospital

Maida Vale Hospital for Nervous Diseases, Maida Vale, W9. Opened as Hospital for Epilepsy and Paralysis and other Diseases of the Nervous System, 1866; renamed 1937.

clinical records 1900-49; minute books 1883-1948 (Hospital)
Annual reports 1897-1947 (LMA: SC/PPS)

Margaret Street Hospital for Consumption, Margaret Street, Cavendish Square, W1. Opened as Margaret Street Hospital for Consumption and Diseases of the Chest, 1847; renamed 1908.

Annual reports 1898-1906-20 (LMA: SC/PPS)

Marie Curie Hospital for Cancer and Allied Diseases, Fitzjohn's Avenue, NW3. Opened 1930 as Marie Curie Hospital; renamed 1938; closed 1968.

minute books 1936-68 (Wellcome Institute)
Annual reports 1929-47 (LMA: SC/PPS)

Maudsley Hospital, Denmark Hill, SE5. Opened as The Maudsley Military Hospital, 1915; The Maudsley Neurological Clearing Hospital 1919-21; renamed 1923. Some clinical records retained at Hospital.

minute books 1908-48 (Bethlem Royal Hospital, Archives and Museum Department)
minute books 1919-48; annual reports 1924-36 (LMA)

Medical Mission of the Good Shepherd and Babies Home, Harman Street, Shoreditch, E1.
Annual reports 1921-33 (LMA: SC/PPS)

Memorial Cottage Hospital, Mildmay Park, N1.

Annual reports 1897-1919 (LMA: SC/PPS)

Memorial Hospital, Shooters Hill, Woolwich, SE18. Opened as Woolwich and District War Memorial Hospital 1888; also Woolwich and Plumstead Cottage Hospital; renamed Woolwich and District Hospital Association War Memorial Hospital 1931; Memorial Hospital, 1938.

A&D 1927-48; minute books 1927-48 (Hospital)

Annual reports 1902-44 (LMA: SC/PPS)

Metropolitan Ear, Nose and Throat Hospital, Marloes Road, W8. Opened 1838 in Grafton Street; from 1912-42 in Fitzroy Square, W1.

clinical records 1950-66; minute books 1875-1959 (Hospital)
Annual reports 1903-47 (LMA: SC/PPS)

Metropolitan Fever and Smallpox Hospitals at Homerton see Eastern Hospital

Metropolitan Free Hospital, Kingsland Road, E8. Founded 1836 in Carey Street as Metropolitan Free Hospital; moved 1850 to Devonshire Square, Bishopsgate 1850; moved to Kingsland Road, 1876; renamed Metropolitan Hospital 1886; closed 1976.

A&D 1909-77; clinical records 1936-77; minute books 1836-1977; staff records 1903-38 (St Bartholomew's Hospital Archives)
Annual reports 1897-1946 (LMA: SC/PPS)

Metropolitan Smallpox Hospital at Hampstead, NW3.

Annual reports 1876-78 (LMA: SC/PPS)

Middlesex Hospital and Cancer Wing, Mortimer Street and Nassan Street, W1. Opened 1745; Nassan Street closed 1929.

A&D 1737-1985; clinical records 1854-1987; minute books 1737-1985; staff records 1867-1974 (Hospital)
Annual reports 1903-47 (LMA: SC/PPS)

Mildmay Mission Cottage Hospital, Newington Green Road, N1. Opened 1883 as Mildmay Memorial Cottage Hospital; renamed 1908; closed 1958.

A&D 1971-82; minute books 1898-1982 (Royal London Hospital Archives Centre)
minute books 1897-1948; annual reports 1898-1947 (LMA: H33/MM)

Mile End Hospital see London Hospital

Mile End Old Town Infirmary see London Hospital

Mile End Old Town Workhouse see London Hospital

Miller General Hospital, Greenwich High Road, SE10. Opened as Kent Dispensary, 1783 in The Broadway, Deptford; renamed Royal Kent Dispensary, 1837; moved 1855 to Greenwich High Road; renamed Miller Memorial Hospital, 1884; renamed Miller Hospital, 1908

A&R 1904-45; minute books 1783-1964; staff records 1933-51 (LMA: H5/M); annual reports 1897-1947 (LMA: SC/PPS)

Moorfields Eye Hospital, City Road, EC1. Opened 1804 in Charterhouse Square; in Moorfields 1821-99. Also known as Royal London Opthalmic Hospital.

Annual reports 1897-1945 (LMA: SC/PPS)

Mothers' Hospital of the Salvation Army, Lower Clapton Road, E5. Opened 1884 as Ivy House (Maternity) Hospital, Mare Street; moved 1913 and renamed Mothers Hospital 1914; renamed Mothers' Hospital of the Salvation Army, 1922; closed 1986.

A&D 1940-86; clinical records 1913-84; minute books 1862-1986 (St Bartholomew's Hospital Archives)
Annual reports 1902, 1912-47 (LMA: SC/PPS)

Mothers' Lying-In Home see East End Maternity Hospital

Mount Vernon Hospital and Radium Institute, Portland Place, NW1. Opened 1860 as North London Hospital for Consumption and Diseases of the Chest; renamed 1901 Mount Vernon Hospital for Consumption; again renamed 1919.

clinical records 1942-48; minute books 1920-87 (Hospital)
Annual reports 1897-1947 (LMA: SC/PPS)

National Anti-Vivisection Hospital see Battersea General Hospital

National Dental Hospital see Dental Hospital

National Heart Hospital, Westmoreland Street, W1. Opened 1857 as Hospital for Diseases of the Heart in Margaret Street; moved to Newman Street, Oxford Street, c1869 and Westmoreland Street, 1874 clinical records 1907-63; minute books 1902-47 (LMA: H25); annual reports 1902-47 (LMA: SC/PPS) minute books 1868-1971 (Hospital)

National Hospital for Neurology and Neurosurgery, Queen Square, WC1. Opened 1859.

minute books 1859-1948 (Hospital)

National Hospital Queen Square for the Relief and Cure of Diseases of the Nervous System, Queen Square, Bloomsbury, WC1. Opened 1859; known as National Hospital for the Relief and Cure of the Paralysed and Epileptic 1904-25; closed 1948.

Annual reports 1871, 1897-1946 (LMA: SC/PPS)

National Orthopaedic Hospital see Royal National Orthopaedic Hospital

National Temperance Hospital, Hampstead Road, NW1. Opened 1873 as London Temperance Hospital; renamed 1930.

A&D 1874-1981; minute books 1871-1981; staff records 1940-70 (Hospital) Annual reports 1898-1947 (LMA: SC/PPS)

New Cross Hospital, Avonley Road, SE14. Opened 1877 as Deptford Hospital; South Eastern Fever Hospital 1885-1948; New Cross General Hospital 1949-64.

A&D 1897-1916; staff records 1877-1935; minute books 1873-1970 (LMA); annual reports 1879-81 (LMA: SC/PPS)

New End Hospital, New End, Hampstead, NW3. Opened 1800 as Hampstead Union Workhouse; New End House 1915-22; renamed 1922; closed 1986

A&D 1920-36; minute books 1883-1948; staff records 1883-1923 (LMA)

New Hospital for Women see Elizabeth Garrett Anderson Hospital

Nightingale Training School. Started at St Thomas' Hospital in 1860. (LMA: H1/ST/NTS). See *The Nightingale Training School, St Thomas' Hospital 1860-1960* (anon, 1960).

A&D 1860-1966; register of nurses 1875-1942

Northcourt Hospital and Home for Sick Children see Hospital and Home for Incurable Children

North Eastern Hospital for Children see Queen Elizabeth Hospital for Children

North London Hospital see University College Hospital (Main Wing)

North London Hospital for Consumption and Diseases of the Chest see Mount Vernon Hospital and Radium Institute

North Western Hospital, Lawn Road, Hampstead, NW3. Opened 1870 as Hampstead Asylum; renamed Hampstead Hospital, 1876; renamed North Western Fever Hospital, 1885; merged 1948 in Royal Free Hospital)

A&D 1896-1948; clinical records 1896-1948; minute books 1868-1948 (LMA: H35/NW)
minute books 1887-1973; clinical records 1948-73; staff records 1887-1923 (Royal Free Hospital Archives Centre)

North West London Hospital, Kentish Town Road, Haverstock Hill, NW5. Opened 1878 as North West Hospital for Diseases of Women and Children; renamed 1879; closed 1907.

minute books 1878-1907 (Royal Free Hospital Archives Centre)
Annual reports 1898-1906 (LMA: SC/PPS)

Norwood and District Cottage Hospital, Hermitage Road, Upper Norwood, SE19. Opened 1880 as Norwood Cottage Hospital; renamed 1921; closed 1983.

minute books 1902-47 (LMA)

Nuffield House, London Bridge, SE1. Opened 1948; closed 1982.

minute books 1935-49 (LMA: H9/GY/NH)

Opthalmic Hospital see Royal Eye Hospital

Oxygen Hospital, Fitzroy Square, W1. Opened 1896. Now closed.
Annual reports 1901, 1903-04 (LMA: SC/PPS)

Paddington Green Children's Hospital, Paddington Green, W2. Opened 1883.

A&D 1887-1977; minute books 1887-1977; annual reports 1897-1947 (LMA: H30)
minute books 1882-1971 (St Mary's Hospital Archives)

Paddington Hospital and Paddington Infirmary see St Mary's Hospital

Park Fever Hospital and Park Hospital see Hither Green Hospital

Poplar and Stepney Sick Asylum see St Andrew's Hospital

Poplar Hospital, East India Dock Road, Blackwall, E14. Opened 1855 as Poplar Hospital for Accidents; renamed 1937; closed 1974.

minute books 1858-1964 (Royal London Hospital Archives)
Annual reports 1898-1947 (LMA: SC/PPS)

Princess Beatrice Hospital, Old Brompton Road, SW5. Opened 1887 as Queen's Jubilee Hospital in Gloucester Terrace; moved by 1894 to Old Brompton Road; renamed 1907 as Kensington General Hospital and in 1909 as Kensington and Fulham General Hospital; renamed 1921; closed 1978.
minute books 1842-1972; annual reports 1898-1947 (LMA: H4/PB)

Princess Elizabeth of York Hospital for Children see East London Hospital for Children

Princess Louise Hospital for Children, St Quintin Avenue, Kensington, W10. Opened as Kensington Dispensary and Children's Hospital 1840 in Church Street, Kensington.

minute books 1948-71 (St Mary's Hospital Archives)
Annual reports 1902-47 (LMA: SC/PPS)

Priory of St Mary of Bethlehem see Bethlem Royal Hospital

Putney Hospital, Lower Road, SW15. Opened 1904.
See: Souvenir of Putney Hospital Fete 1934 which includes a history
Registers of patients 1935-78; minute books 1905-72; matrons' report book 1959-69; registers of nurses 1912-37; bequests 1911-45; postcards 1935; financial records 1912-45 (LMA: H2/PY); annual reports 1913-47 (LMA: SC/PPS)
A&D 1935-70; clinical records 1950; minute books 1912-72 (Hospital)

Queen Adelaide Fund (LMA: H11/QAF) Founded 1835 to assist patients released from mental instututions. There are a variety of records in the LMA; those of greatest interest are the books of recommendations 1842-1933.

Queen Alexandra Military Hospital, SW1. Closed.

Queen Charlotte's Maternity Hospital, Goldhawk Road, W6. Founded as the General Lying-in Hospital in 1739 in Marylebone Road, NW1.

A&D 1952-54; examinations as to married status 1816; registers of patients 1809-22, 1827-53, 1857-1949; midwives' registers of cases 1934-43; operations 1953-66; minute books 1838-1984; list of midwives 1940-45; registers of pupils 1888-97, 1908-25, 1955-56, 1972-73; legacies 1894-1983; visitors 1899-1935 (LMA: H27/QC); annual reports 1897-1947, 1950-53 (LMA: SC/PPS)
A&D 1816-64; minute books 1809-1984; staff records 1927-60 (Hospital)

Queen Elizabeth Hospital for Children, Hackney Road, Bethnal Green, E2. Opened 1867 in Virginia Road as Dispensary for Women and Children; moved to Hackney Road, Shoreditch in 1868 as North Eastern Hospital for Children 1868 and moved to Bethnal Green, 1870. Queen's Hospital for Children until 1941.

A&D 1893-1990; clinical records 1893-1990; minute books 1868-1990; staff records 1897-1990 (Hospital)
minute books 1868-1963 (Royal London Hospital Archives Centre)
Annual reports 1897-1947 (LMA: SC/PPS)

Queen Mary's House, Heath Street, Hampstead, NW3. Opened 1919 in North End Road as Queen Mary's Maternity Home; renamed 1922.

minute books 1914-72 (Royal London Hospital Archives Centre)
minute books 1920-60 (Royal Free Hospital Archives Centre)

Queen Mary's (Roehampton) Hospital, Roehampton Lane, SW15. Opened in Ducane Road, 1915 for convalescent service personnel; moved 1925.

minute books 1915-71; annual reports 1928-69; visitors 1915-68; staff records 1961-69 (LMA: H2/QM)

Queen's Hospital for Children see Queen Elizabeth Hospital for Children

Queen's Jubilee Hospital see Princess Beatrice Hospital

Ross Institute and Hospital for Tropical Diseases, Putney Heath, SW15.

Annual reports 1926-29 (LMA: SC/PPS)

Royal Brompton National Heart and Lung Hospital, Fulham Road, SW3. Opened as Hospital for Consumption and Diseases of the Chest, in Chelsea, 1842; renamed 1846.

A&D 1885-1933; staff records 1887-1951; clinical records 1912-57; Administrative records 1841-1980 (Brompton Hospital)
Clinical records 1862-1933 (Royal College of Physicians of London)
Annual reports 1897-1947 (LMA: SC/PPS)

Royal Cancer Hospital see Royal Marsden Hospital

Royal Chest Hospital, City Road, EC1. Opened 1814 as Infirmary for Asthma, Consumption and other Pulmonary Diseases in Union Street, Spitalfields; moved to Artillery Street, Spitalfields, 1833 and to City Road, 1850; renamed 1859 Royal Infirmary for Diseases of the Chest; 1867 Royal Hospital for Diseases of the Chest; renamed 1919; closed 1954. See: History of the Royal Chest Hospital (N.H. Chuster, 1955)

minute books 1825-1940; annual reports 1827-1920; visitors 1886-1921 (LMA: H33/RCH)

Royal Dental Hospital, Leicester Square, WC2. Opened 1858 as Dental Hospital of London; renamed 1900; closed 1985.

A&D 1870-1980; minute books 1859-1980 (Hospital)

operations 1933-37; minute books 1858-1986; annual reports 1859-1983 (LMA: H42/RD)

Royal Ear Hospital, Huntley Street, WC1. Opened in Carlisle Street, 1816 as Dispensary for Diseases of the Ear; moved to Dean Street, 1820; renamed 1822 as Royal Dispensary for Diseases of the Ear; moved to Huntley Street in 1876; renamed Royal Ear Hospital, 1920.

minute books 1837-1947 (University College Hospital)
Annual reports 1897-1912 (LMA: SC/PPS)

Royal Eye Hospital, St George's Circus, SE1. Opened 1857 as South London Opthalmic Hospital; renamed Surrey Opthalmic Hospital, 1860, The Opthalmic Hospital, 1863 and the Royal Eye Hospital, 1869; closed 1980.

A&D 1861-1972; clinical records 1893-1958; minute books 1857-1980; staff records 1956-63 (LMA: H15/RE); annual reports 1898-1947 (LMA: SC/PPS)

Royal Free Hospital, Pond Street, NW3. Opened 1828 as London General Institution for the Gratuitous Cure of Malignant Diseases in Greville Street, Hatton Garden; renamed Free Hospital 1835; renamed Royal Free Hospital, 1837; moved to Gray's Inn Road, 1845; moved to Pond Street, 1973-79.

Annual reports 1897-1946 (LMA: SC/PPS)

Royal Free Hospital Liverpool Road Branch, Liverpool Road, Islington,, N1. Opened 1802 as Institution for the cure and prevention of contagious fevers; London Fever Hospital 1849-1948; closed 1974.

A&D 1837-1937; clinical records 1824-1962; minute books 1801-1960; staff records 1917-60 (Royal Free Hospital Archives Centre)
Annual reports 1898-1946 (LMA: SC/PPS)

Royal Hospital, Royal Hospital Road, Chelsea, SW3. Opened 1692. Colloquially known as Chelsea Pensioners' Hospital.

A&D 1691-1920; minute books 1691-1974 (PRO)

Royal Hospital and Home, West Hill, Putney, SW15. Opened as Royal Hospital and Home for Incurables in Carshalton, Surrey, 1854; moved to Putney, 1857; renamed Hospital and Home for Incurables, 1919; renamed Royal Hospital and Home, 1987.

A&D 1854-1994; clinical records 1854-1994; minute books 1854-1994 (Hospital)
Annual report 1922 (LMA: SC/PPS)

Royal Hospital for Children and Women see Royal Waterloo Hospital for Children and Women

Royal Hospital for Diseases of the Chest see Royal Chest Hospital

Royal Infirmary for Children and Women see Royal Waterloo Hospital for Children and Women

Royal Infirmary for Diseases of the Chest see Royal Chest Hospital

Royal Kent Dispensary see Miller General Hospital

Royal London Homeopathic Hospital, Great Ormond Street and Queen Square, WC1. Opened 1849 as London Homeopathic Hospital; renamed c1948.

A&D 1933-81; clinical records 1848-94; minute books 1848-1984; staff records (Hospital)

Annual reports 1897-1947 (LMA: SC/PPS)

Royal London Opthalmic Hospital see Moorfields Eye Hospital

Royal Marsden Hospital, Fulham Road, SW3. Founded as The Cancer Hospital, 1851; by 1940 it was the Royal Cancer Hospital; renamed Royal Marsden Hospital, 1955.

A&D 1886-1963; clinical records 1886-1953; minute books 1816-1979 (Hospital)
Annual reports 1869, 1897-1947 (LMA: SC/PPS)

Royal Masonic Hospital, Ravenscourt Park, W6. Opened 1933; closed 1996.

Royal National Orthopaedic Hospital, Bolsover Street, W1. Opened 1838; by 1866 National Orthopaedic Hospital; also known as City Orthopaedic Hospital; renamed 1905 when in Great Portland Street; moved to Bolsover Street, 1984. See: History of the Royal National Orthopaedic Hospital (J.A. Cholmeley, 1985)

A&D 1941-42, 1970-75, 1986-88, 1990; casualties 1956-89; journals 1906-48; minute books 1897-1990; annual reports 1897-1947 (LMA: H8/B)

Royal National Throat Nose and Ear Hospital, Judd Street, WC1. Opened as Central London Throat, Nose and Ear Hospital in Grays Inn Road, 1874; renamed c1948.

minute books 1900-01 (Hospital)
Annual reports 1898-1939 (LMA: SC/PPS)

Royal Naval College, Romney Road, Greenwich, SE10.

A&D 1705-1864; burials 1844-1981; minute books 1695-1871; staff records 1819 (PRO; various ADM classes)

Royal Northern Hospital, Holloway Road, N7. Opened in York Road, King's Cross as Great Northern Hospital, 1856; moved to Portland Street, 1862 and Holloway Road 1864; Great Northern Central Hospital 1884-1921.
See: The Royal Northern Hospital (C.O. Jewesbury, 1956)

A&D 1905-91; births 1943-57; deaths 1939-91; matron's reports 1905-50; minute books 1856-1991; annual reports 1864, 1870, 1878, 1884, 1889, 1894-1948; registers of nurses 1873-91, 1905-09; staff records 1899-1963 (LMA: H33/RN)

Royal Opthalmic Hospital see Moorfields Eye Hospital

Royal Orthopaedic Hospital for Club Foot, Spinal and other Deformities, Oxford Street, W1. Opened 1838 as Royal Orthopaedic Hospital for the Cure of Club Foot, Lateral Curvature of the Spine, and all other Contractions and Deformities; closed 1905.

Annual reports 1897-1904 (LMA: SC/PPS)

Royal Universal Dispensary for Children see Royal Waterloo Hospital for Children and Women

Royal Universal Infirmary for Children see Royal Waterloo Hospital for Children and Women

Royal Waterloo Hospital for Children and Women, Waterloo Bridge Road, SE1. Founded 1816 as Universal Dispensary for Children in St Andrew's Hill, Doctors' Commons; changed 1821 to Royal Universal Dispensary for Children; In 1824 new building on corner of Waterloo Bridge Road and Stamford Street, Lambeth; renamed Royal Universal Infirmary for Children 1843 and in 1852 to Royal Infirmary for Children and Women. In 1875 became Royal Hospital for Children and Women and in 1903 Royal Waterloo Hospital for Children and Women. Closed 1976. See: The Origin and Progress of the Royal Hospital for Children and Women, Waterloo Bridge Road (London, 1899); Prince's Meadows and Poverty Corner, being a short account of Royal Waterloo Hospital for Children and Women, Mrs Molesworth, 1907; The Universal Dispensary for Children (British Medical Journal, 5 May 1979)

A&D 1942-47, 1967-76; minute books 1815-33 (PRO: PRO 30/26) minute books 1832-1949; registers of sick children and women 1816-99; matrons' reports 1912-46; registers of nurses 1890-1923 (LMA: HI/RW); annual reports 1897-1947 (LMA: SC/PPS)

Royal Westminster Ophthalmic Hospital, Broad Street, Holborn, WC2. Opened 1816; closed 1948.

Annual reports 1898-1945 (LMA: SC/PPS)

St Alfege's Hospital see Greenwich District Hospital

St Andrew's Hospital, Devons Road, Bow, E3. Opened as Poplar and Stepney Sick Asylum, 1868; renamed 1921.

minute books 1913-48; staff records 1922-30; annual reports 1913-39 (LMA) A&D 1873-1966; clinical records 1886-1974; minute books 1873-1985; staff records 1961-70 (Royal London Hospital Archives Centre)

St Bartholomew's Hospital, West Smithfield, EC1. Opened 1123.

A&D 1818-1971; clinical records 1826-1985; administrative records 1137-1998; staff records 1645-1974 (St Bartholomew's Hospital Archives and Museum) Annual reports 1902-47 (LMA: SC/PPS)

St Benedict's Hospital, Church Lane, SW17. Opened 1931; closed 1981.

minute books 1930-48 (LMA)

St Charles's Hospital, Exmoor Street, W10. Opened as St Marylebone Infirmary, 1881; renamed St Marylebone Hospital, 1923; renamed, 1930. See St Charles Hospital 1881-1981: a century of service (B. Curle, c1981)

A&D 1891-1943; baptisms 1889-1983; deaths 1884-1934; minute books 1881-1983; staff records 1888-1930 (LMA: H28/SC; StMBG; P84/SCH) clinical records 1950; minute books 1900-70; staff records 1900-44 (Hospital)

St Christopher's Hospital see Fulham Hospital

St Clement's Hospital, Bow Road, E3. Opened as City of London Workhouse, c1849; City of London Infirmary 1877-1913; City of London, Bow Institution 1914-36; St Clement's Hospital 1936-68; renamed London Hospital (St Clement's), 1968; closed 1979.

A&D 1874-1932; minute books 1857-1944 (LMA) A&D 1895-1939; clinical records 1919-30; minute books 1891-1974 (Royal London Hospital Archives Centre)

St Columba's Hospital, Avenue Road, Hampstead, NW3. Opened 1885 as Friedenheim Hospital; also known as the Home of Peace; renamed 1913; closed 1981.

Annual reports 1902-47 (LMA: SC/PPS)

St Francis Cripples' Home see Westminster Children's Hospital

St Francis' Hospital, St Francis Road, SE22. Opened 1892 as Constance Road Institution; renamed 1937; closed 1982. A&D 1894-1931; minute books 1894-1948 (LMA)

St George in the East Hospital, Raine Street, E1. Opened as St George in the East Infirmary, 1844; renamed 1925; closed 1956.

A&D 1871-1925; minute books 1871-1948 (Hospital) minute books 1956 (Royal London Hospital Archives Centre)

St George's Home, Milman's Street, SW10. Opened 1914; closed 1957.

staff records 1902-28; minute books 1902-48 (LMA)

St George's Hospital, Blackshaw Road, SW17. Opened 1733 in Lanesborough House, Knightsbridge; moved to Hyde Park Corner, 1833; moved to SW17, 1980.

A&D 1900-87; clinical records 1965-87; minute books 1733-1987; staff records 1733-1987 (St George's Hospital Medical School Library) Annual reports 1898-1947 (LMA: SC/PPS)

St George's Union Infirmary see St Stephen's Hospital

St Giles' Hospital, St Giles, Camberwell, SE5. Opened 1873 as Camberwell Workhouse Infirmary; renamed Camberwell Parish Infirmary, c1910; renamed St Giles' Hospital, 1927.

A&D 1873-1943, 1948-54, 1964-68; births 1874-1954; deaths 1874-1951; casualties 1939-43; creed registers 1875-

1943; index of patients 1879-95; 1936-53; minute books 1873-1968 (LMA: H38/SG)

A&D 1873-1954; minute books 1873-1954 (Hospital)

St James' Hospital, Sarsfield Road, Balham, SW12. Opened as St James' Infirmary, 1909; renamed 1922.

A&D 1921-23; baptisms 1911-17, 1930-82; minute books 1910-48 (LMA: H46/SJ; P95/MMG)

St John's Hospital, St John's Hill, SW11. Wandsworth and Clapham Poor Law Union Workhouse operated from 1836. The hospital opened in 1870 as Wandsworth and Clapham Union Infirmary; renamed St John's Hill Infirmary, 1920, St John's Hospital, 1922; closed 1990.

A&D 1872-3, 1881-3, 1943-56; creed registers 1872-75, 1904-07; births 1866-86, 1931-36; deaths 1866-86, 1933-37, 1942-48; settlement examinations 1898-1928; operations 1930-64; minute books 1870-1978; staff records 1931-73 (LMA: H29/SJ; WaBG)

St John's Hospital, Morden Hill, Lewisham, SE13. Opened 1884; closed 1983.

clinical records 1930-76; minute books 1870-1969 (Lewisham Local Studies Centre)

Annual reports 1902-47 (LMA: SC/PPS)

St John's Hospital for Diseases of the Skin, Lisle Street, WC2. Opened in Church Street, Leicester Square in 1863; moved to Leicester Square, 1865 and Lisle Street, 1887.

minute books 1875-1977 (LMA: H15/SJ); annual reports 1899-1947 (LMA: SC/PPS)
minute books 1897-1976; staff records 1949-50 (Hospital)

St Leonard's Hospital, Nuttall Street, Kingsland Road, N1. Opened 1777 as St Leonard Shoreditch Workhouse Infirmary; renamed Shoreditch Infirmary, 1872; renamed St Leonard's Hospital, 1920; in-patients' department closed 1948.

A&D 1869-1940; minute books 1869-1948 (LMA: H19/SL)
A&D 1898-1967; clinical records 1885-1969; minute books 1898-1976 (St Bartholomew's Hospital Archives and Museum)

St Luke's Hospital, Sydney Street, SW3. Opened as Chelsea Workhouse Infirmary, 1874; renamed 1925; closed 1974.

A&D 1899-1902; minute books 1872-1950 (LMA: H17/SL)

St Luke's Hospital for the Dying see Hereford Lodge

St Luke's Woodside Hospital, Woodside Avenue, Muswell Hill, N10. Opened 1930 as Woodside Nerve Hospital; renamed 1940 as St Luke's Woodside Hospital for Functional Nervous Disorders.

A&D 1751-53; clinical records 1858-1920; minute books 1750-1962; staff records 1925-38 (Hospital)
Annual reports 1970-73 (LMA: SC/PPS)

St Margaret's Hospital, Leighton Road, NW5. Opened 1918; closed 1947.

minute books 1918-48 (Hospital)

St Mark's Hospital for Diseases of the Rectum and Colon, City Road, Finsbury, EC1. Opened in Aldersgate Street as Infirmary for Relief of the Poor Afflicted With Fistula and other Diseases of the Rectum, 1835; moved to Charterhouse Square, 1837; moved to City Road and renamed St Mark's Hospital for Fistula and other Diseases of the Rectum, 1854; renamed again 1909; amalgamated with St Bartholomew's, 1972-4.

A&D 1900-85; clinical records 1913-86; minute books 1840-1996; staff records 1840-1981 (St Bartholomew's Hospital Archives and Museum)
Annual reports 1898-1947 (LMA: SC/PPS)

St Mary Abbot's Hospital, Marloes Road, W8. Opened as Kensington Infirmary, 1892; renamed 1922; closed 1992.

A&D 1872-1958; births 1872-1907, 1930-37, 1944-52; baptisms in chapel 1877-1920; deaths 1886- 1937, 1942-54; creed registers 1875-83, 1887-1932; maternity registers 1932-44; minute books 1872-1991; staff records 1891-1953, 1968-70 (LMA: H17/SL)

See: *From Workhouse to Hospital. The Story of St Mary Abbots Hospital, Kensington* (B. Hughes, 1991)

St Marylebone and Western General Dispensary, Cosway Street, Marylebone Road, NW1. Opened 1785 as St Marylebone Dispensary in Queen Anne Street, East Wells Street; in Margaret Street 1787-1804, Welbeck Street 1804-1925; also premises in Marylebone Lane 1894-1936; renamed 1936.

minute books 1785-1950 (City of Westminster Archives Centre)

St Marylebone Hospital and St Marylebone Infirmary see St Charles's Hospital

St Mary's Dispensary in Bryanston Square, St Marylebone see Elizabeth Garrett Anderson Hospital

St Mary's Hospital, Harrow Road, W9. Opened as Paddington Infirmary, 1886; renamed Paddington Hospital, 1932; renamed St Mary's Hospital, 1968.

A&D 1886-89; minute books 1883-1953 (LMA)
A&D 1917-50; minute books 1917-50 (Hospital)

St Mary's Hospital, Praed Street, W2. Opened 1845.

A&D 1906-84; clinical records 1882-1930; minute books 1849-1984 (Hospital)

minute books 1912-45 (Wellcome Institute)

Annual reports 1897-1953 (LMA: SC/PPS)

St Mary's Islington Infirmary and St Mary Islington Hospital see Whittington Hospital

St Matthew's Hospital, Shepherdess Walk, N1. Opened 1870 as Holborn and Finsbury Workhouse; renamed Holborn and Finsbury Institution, 1930, St Matthew's Hospital, 1936. Closed 1986.

A&D 1860-1986; deaths 1939-40, 1970-86; lunatics 1922-24; registers of children 1914-31; creed registers 1869-89, 1900-15, 1935-40; clinical records 1879-1954; minute books 1879-1986; annual reports 1950-60; staff records 1925-58 (LMA: H19/SM; Ho.BG; LCC/MIN)

St Nicholas' Hospital, Tewson Road, Plumstead, SE18. Opened 1872 as Woolwich Union Infirmary; later Woolwich Union Plumstead and District Hospital.

A&D 1874-1984; minute books 1874-1984 (LMA: H20)

St Olave's Hospital, Lower Road, SE16. Opened 1876 as Rotherhithe Workhouse, later Bermondsey and Rotherhithe Infirmary, later Bermondsey and Rotherhithe Hospital; closed 1985.

A&D 1848-1959; births 1942-54; baptisms 1914-67; deaths 1935-38, 1941-59; creed registers 1892-96, 1901-03, 1905-07, 1913-18, 1923-32; staff records 1876-1930; minute books 1848-1959 (LMA: H3/OLA; P71/ALL)

St Pancas Hospital, St Pancras Way, NW1. The Hospital originated as St Pancras Workhouse, which opened an infirmary in about 1885. Opened 1903 as St Pancras Infirmary; renamed 1922.

A&D 1902-39; baptisms 1857-82, 1892-1940; minute books 1867-1948; punishment book 1914-37; staff records 1889-1930 (LMA: H31/SP; St P.BG; P90/PANI)
clinical records 1940-53; minute books 1857-1958 (Hospital)

St Pancras' North Infirmary see Highgate Hospital

St Paul's Hospital for Diseases (including Cancer) of the Genito-Urinary organs and skin, Endell Street, WC2. Opened 1897 in Red Lion Square, WC2; moved 1923.

Annual reports 1908-47 (LMA: SC/PPS)

St Peter's Hospital, Fulbourne Street, E1. Opened 1842 as Whitechapel Union Infirmary; renamed 1924; closed 1948.

A&D 1853-1932; minute books 1853-1947; annual reports 1898-1947 (LMA)

St Peter's Hospital, Henrietta Street, W1. Opened 1867.

Annual reports 1898-1947 (LMA: SC/PPS)

St Philip's Hospital, Sheffield Street, WC2. Opened 1920 as Sheffield Street Hospital; renamed c1951.

A&D 1909-13; minute books 1909-48 (LMA)

St Saviour's Hospital for Ladies of Limited Means, Osnaburgh Street, Regent's Park, NW1. Opened 1872; closed 1948.

Annual reports 1897-1941 (LMA: SC/PPS)

St Saviour's Union Infirmary see Dulwich Hospital

St Stephen's Hospital, Fulham Road, SW10. Opened 1878 as St George's Union Infirmary; renamed Fulham Road Infirmary, 1915; also known as City of Westminster Hospital from 1924.

A&D 1934-62; minute books 1878-1971 (LMA: H17/SS)

St Thomas' Hospital, Lambeth Palace Road, SE1. Opened 1200 in Borough High Street; moved to Surrey Gardens, Newington, 1862 and to Lambeth Palace Road, 1871. See: 'An Historical Account of St Thomas's Hospital' (B. Golding, 1819); 'The History of St Thomas's Hospital' (F.G. Parsons, 3 vols, 1933-36); 'The Story of St Thomas's' (C. Graves, 1947); 'St Thomas' Hospital' (E.M. McInnes, 1963). Also 'St Thomas' Hospital, London, and its Archives' (E.M. McInnes in Journal of the Society of Archivists vol.1 no.10 Oct 1959.

A&D 1672-1865, 1870-1, 1890-1929, 1933-57; Baptisms 1880-1946; Deaths 1763-1964; clinical records (few only) 1878-1936; minute books 1557-1959; annual reports 1894-1990; staff records 1844-1919, 1941-56 (LMA: H1/ST) A&D 1803-21; minute books 1803-21 (Southwark Local Studies Library)

St Thomas' Babies' Hostel see Child Psychiatric Day Hospital

St Thomas Cornwall Babies' Hostel see Child Psychiatric Day Hospital

Samaritan Hospital for Women, Marylebone Road, NW1. Opened 1847 as Samaritan Free Hospital for Women and Children; renamed Samaritan Free Hospital for Women, 1902; renamed Samaritan Hospital for Women, c1950

A&D 1915-71; clinical records 1920-48; minute books 1854-1971 (Hospital) Annual reports 1897-1947 (LMA: SC/PPS)

Santa Claus Home for Sick Children, Cholmeley Park, Highgate, N6. Opened 1891; closed 1954.

minute books 1891-1953; annual reports 1902-47 (LMA: H33/SC)

Sheffield Street Hospital see St Philip's Hospital

Shoreditch Infirmary see St Leonard's Hospital

South Eastern District Hospital, Old Kent Road, SE1.

Annual reports 1882-85 (LMA: SC/PPS)

South Eastern Fever Hospital see New Cross Hospital

South Eastern Hospital for Children see Children's Hospital

Southern Districts Hospital see South Western Hospital

South London Hospital for Women and Children, Southside, Clapham Common, SW4. Opened as South London Hospital for Women in Newington Causeway, 1912; moved to Clapham, 1916; renamed, c1940; closed 1984.

minute books 1911-87; staff records 1916-56; annual reports 1912-47 (LMA: H24/SLW)
minute books and staff records (Lambeth Archives Department)

South London Opthalmic Hospital see Royal Eye Hospital
Southwark Hospital see Dulwich Hospital

South Western Hospital, Landor Road, SW9. Opened as Southern Districts Hospital, 1867; renamed Stockwell Fever Hospital, 1885; South Western Fever Hospital 1885-1948.

A&D 1871-1906; minute books 1868-1990; staff records 1889-1921 (LMA: H15/SW); annual reports 1871-84 (LMA: SC/PPS)

Spinal Hospital, Portland Road, W11. Closed 1862.

minute books 1860-62 (LMA: H33/RN)

Springfield Hospital, Glenburnie Road, SW17. Opened 1841 as Surrey County Lunatic Asylum; renamed Wandsworth Asylum, 1889; later Springfield Asylum; renamed Springfield Hospital, c1918.

A&D 1841-1980; clinical records 1846-1960; minute books 1841-1990; staff records 1935-51 (LMA: H46/SP)
A&D 1841-1959; clinical records 1880-1964; minute books 1841-1963; staff records 1882-1963 (Hospital)
clinical records 1849-1938; minute books 1838-89 (Surrey History Centre: Q55/6; 6367)

Stockwell Fever Hospital see South Western Hospital

Stoke Newington Home Hospital for Women see Invalid Asylum and Stoke Newington Home Hospital for Women

Streatham Babies Hospital, Leigham Court Road, Streatham, SW16.

Annual reports 1921-39 (LMA: SC/PPS)

Surrey County Lunatic Asylum see Springfield Hospital

Surrey Opthalmic Hospital see Royal Eye Hospital

Sydenham Babies Hospital see Children's Hospital

Thavies Inn Infirmary, Robin Hood Court, Holborn, EC4. Opened 1901 as City of London Workhouse 1901; renamed City of London Union Infirmary 1914; renamed 1927; absorbed by Sheffield Street Hospital, 1931.

A&D 1889-1932; minute books 1889-1932 (LMA)

Tooting Bec Hospital, Tooting Bec, SW17. Opened 1903 as Tooting Bec Asylum.
See *History of Tooting Bec Hospital* (S. Simmons, 1995)

Deaths 1944-63; A&D 1930-64; Creed registers 1938-47; registers of patients 1960-88; post-mortem registers 1932-59; minute books 1948-67; medical superintendent's report books 1903-05, 1909-11; visitors 1903-61; staff records 1902-65
A&D 1903-60; minute books 1903-63; staff records 1903-41 (Hospital)

Universal Dispensary for Children see Royal Waterloo Hospital for Children and Women

University College Hospital (Main Wing), Gower Street, WC1. Opened 1833 as North London Hospital; renamed 1836.

A&D 1942-48; clinical records 1834-1947; staff records 1948-61; minute books 1824-1974 (Hospital)
minute books 1897-1962 (LMA)

University College Hospital (Private Patient's Wing), Grafton Way, WC1. Opened 1937.

A&D 1937-48; minute books 1937-48 (Bloomsbury Health Authority)

Annual reports 1897-1962 (LMA: SC/PPS)

Victoria Home for Children, Tite Street, Chelsea, SW3. Opened 1866; closed 1948. A commemorative history 1866-1964 is to be found in LMA at H1/ST.Lib/22.

Annual reports 1873, 1898-1947 (LMA: SC/PPS)

Wandsworth and Clapham Union Infirmary see St John's Hospital

Wandsworth Asylum see Springfield Hospital

Wandworth Maternity Hospital see Weir Maternity Hospital

Weir Maternity Hospital, Weir Road, SW12. Opened 1911 as Weir Hospital in Grove Road, Balham; also known as Wandworth Maternity Hospital.

minute books 1919-57 (St George's Hospital Medical School Library)
Annual reports 1920-47 (LMA: SC/PPS)

West End Hospital for Nervous Diseases, Welbeck Street, NW1. Opened 1878 as West End Hospital for Diseases of the Nervous System, Paralysis and Epilepsy; renamed 1915.

Annual reports 1898-1947 (LMA: SC/PPS)

Western General Dispensary, Cosway Street, Marylebone Road, NW1. Opened 1830 in Lisson Grove South, Marylebone Road; moved 1873; closed 1936.
minute books 1830-1936 (City of Westminster Archives Centre)

Western Hospital, Seagrave Road, SW10. Opened 1877 as Fulham Hospital; renamed Western Fever Hospital 1885; renamed 1948; closed 1979.

A&D 1897-1906; minute books 1872-1948 (LMA)
minute books 1877-1951 (Charing Cross Hospital)

A&D 1963-79; minute books 1963-79 (Hammersmith and Fulham Archives and Local History Centre)

Western Hospital for Fistula, Piles and Other Diseases of the Rectum see Gordon Hospital

Western Opthalmic Hospital, Marylebone Road and Circus Road, NW1. Opened 1856.

A&D 1929-67; clinical records 1939-72; minute books 1870-1963 (Hospital)
Annual reports 1898-1947 (LMA: SC/PPS)

Western Skin Hospital, Hampstead Road, NW1. Opened 1851; closed 1948.

Annual reports 1908-37 (LMA: SC/PPS)

West London Hospital, Hammersmith Road, W6. Opened 1856.

A&D 1899-1976; clinical records 1915-76; minute books 1856-1993; staff records 1874-1969 (Hammersmith and Fulham Archives and Local History Centre)

clinical records 1923 (Charing Cross Hospital)

Annual reports 1897-1947 (LMA: SC/PPS)

Westminster Children's Hospital, Vincent Square, SW1. Opened 1903 in Hampstead as St Francis Cripples' Home; renamed 1903 The Infants' Hospital; moved 1907; renamed Westminster Children's Hospital, 1946.

A&D 1961-75; registers of patients 1907-74; registers of casualties 1937-39; 1947-81; post-mortems 1923-51; casebooks 1921-39, 1949-50; minute books 1906-72; annual reports 1903-45; visitors 1907-60 (LMA: H2/WCH); annual reports 1907-45 (LMA: SC/PPS)

Westminster Hospital, Dean Ryle Street, SW1. Opened 1720 in Petty France as Westminster Infirmary for the Sick and Needy; renamed 1770; new building in Broad Sanctuary, 1832, and again in St John's Gardens, 1939. Chartham Park Convalescent Home presented to Hospital in 1946. Various other Hospitals affiliated 1946-48. Wolfson School of Nursing opened 1960. From 1948, part of South West Metropolitan Region; 1974 part of North West Thames Regional Health Authority; 1982, Riverside District Health Authority.

See: Westminster Hospital – an outline of its History (W.G. Spencer, 1924; Westminster Hospital 1719-1948 (J. Langdon-Davies, 1952); Westminster Hospital 1716-1966 (J.G. Humble & P. Hansell, 1966, 2nd ed., 1974)
Deaths 1860-78, 1885-1905, 1913-40, 1947-67; post-mortems 1846-53; registers of patients 1733-34, 1933-67, 1972-73; minute books 1716-1969; registers of servants 1827-32, 1849-1955; registers of nurses 1885-90, 1899-1949; staff records 1954-66; photograph 1966; endowments 1868-1940 (LMA: H2/WH); annual reports 1897-1947 (LMA: SC/PPS)

clinical records 1955-75 (Hospital)
minute books 1719-33 (City of Westminster Archives Centre)
clinical records 1929-70 (Wellcome Institute)

Westminster Hospital Urological Centre, Austral Street, SE11. Opened 1911 as All Saint's Hospital; renamed 1916 as All Saint's Hospital for Genito-Urinary Diseases; renamed 1946. Closed c1952. 49/57 Vauxhall Bridge Road, London SW1 from 1911 to 1932 and 91 Finchley Road, London NW8 from 1920 to 1932.

A&D 1914-17; deaths 1938-83; operations 1963-66; matrons' reports 1945-68; minute books 1912-68; annual reports 1911-46; visitors 1914-68; staff records 1919-39 (LMA: H2/AS)

Westminster Infirmary for the Sick and Needy see Westminster Hospital
Westminster New Lying-in Hospital see

General Lying-in Hospital
Whitechapel Union Infirmary see St Peter's Hospital

Whittington Hospital, Highgate Hill, N19. Opened 1900 as St Mary's Islington Infirmary; renamed St Mary Islington Hospital, 1930; renamed Whittington Hospital, 1952.

A&D 1901-29; minute books 1891-1948; staff records 1901-24 (LMA)

Winifred House Invalid Children's Nursing Home, Wray Crescent, Tollington Park, N4. Opened 1890. Moved to Barnet, Hertfordshire, 1937.

A&D 1906-23; staff 1939-72 (LMA: H55/WIN); annual reports 1904-47 (LMA: SC/PPS)

Wolfson School of Nursing see Westminster Hospital

Women's Hospital for Children, Harrow Road, W2. Renamed Roll of Honour Hospital for Children in 1920s.

Annual reports 1913-14, 1920 (LMA: SC/PPS)
Woodside Nerve Hospital see St Luke's Woodside Hospital

Woolwich and District War Memorial Hospital and Woolwich and District Hospital Association War Memorial Hospital see Memorial Hospital
Woolwich and Plumstead Cottage Hospital see Memorial Hospital

Woolwich Union Infirmary see St
Nicholas' Hospital

Woolwich Union Plumstead and District
Hospital see St Nicholas' Hospital

York Clinic, Guy's Hospital, Borough
High Street, SE1. Opened 1948; closed
1982.

minute books 1939-48 (LMA:
H9/GY/YC)

London Hospitals by Postal District

E1 Mile End; St George in the East; Shadwell; Spitalfields; Stepney; Wapping; Whitechapel

E2 Bethnal Green; Shoreditch (part)

E3 Bromley by Bow; Mile End (part); Stratford le Bow

E5 Clapton; Hackney (part)

E8 Dalston; Hackney (part); Homerton (part)

E9 Hackney (part); Homerton (part)

E14 Isle of Dogs; Limehouse; Poplar

EC1 City (North West); Clerkenwell; Holborn

EC2 City (North East)

EC3 City (South East)

EC4 City (South West)

N1 Islington (part); Shoreditch (part)

N4 Highbury (part); Tollington Park

N5 Highbury (part); Highgate (part)

N6 Highgate (part)

N7 Holloway (part); Islington (part)

N16 Stamford Hill (part); Stoke Newington

N17 Stamford Hill (part)

N19 Holloway (part); Islington (part)

NW1 Camden Town; St Marylebone (part); St Pancras

NW2 Cricklewood

NW3 Hampstead (part); Haverstock Hill

NW5 Kentish Town; St Pancras (part)

NW6 GospelOak; Hampstead (part); Kilburn

NW8 St John's Wood; St Marylebone (part)

NW10 Kensal Green

NW11 Golders Green; Hampstead (part)

SE1 Bermondsey (part); Lambeth (part); Southwark

SE2 Abbey Wood

SE3 Blackheath

SE4 Brockley

SE5 Camberwell

SE6 Catford; Rushey Green

SE7 Charlton

SE8 Deptford (part)

SE9 Eltham

SE10 Blackheath (part); Greenwich (part)

SE11 Kennington; Lambeth (part)

SE12 Lewisham (part)

SE13 Hither Green; Lee; Lewisham (part)

SE14 Deptford; Hatcham; New Cross

SE15 Nunhead; Peckham

SE16 Bermondsey (part); Rotherhithe

SE17 Camberwell (part); Walworth (part)

SE18 Plumstead; Woolwich (part)

SE19 Upper Norwood

SE21 Dulwich

SE22 EastDulwich; Peckham Rye

SE23 Brockley; Forest Hill

SE24 Herne Hill

SE26 Sydenham

SE27 West Norwood

SW1 Westminster (part)

SW2 Brixton; Tulse Hill

SW3 Chelsea

SW4 Clapham

SW5 Kensington (part)

SW6 Fulham

SW7 Kensington (part)

SW8 Battersea; Kennington (part); Lambeth (part)

SW9 Brixton (part); Kennington (part)

SW10 Chelsea (part)

SW11 Battersea (part); Clapham (part)

SW12 Balham

SW15 Putney; Roehampton; Wandsworth (part)

SW16 Streatham

SW17 Tooting

SW18 Putney (part); Wandsworth (part)

SW19 Wimbledon Park

W1 St Marylebone (part); St Pancras (part); Westminster (part)

W2 Bayswater; Paddington (part)

W4 Hammersmith (part)

W6 Hammersmith (part)

W8 Kensington (part)

W9 Paddington (part)

W10 Kensal Green; Kensington (part); Ladbroke Grove; Paddington

W11 Kensington (part); Notting Hill

W12 Hammersmith (part)

W14 Kensington (part)

WC1 Holborn (part); St Pancras (part)

WC2 Holborn (part)